This is Daniel Cook
Making Honey

Kids Can Press

This is Daniel Cook.
He likes to go different places,
meet interesting people and
try new things.

Mostly I like to have fun!

Today Daniel is learning about beekeeping.

Here we are!

This is Allan. He's a beekeeper. Beekeepers are farmers. While the bees are busy making honey, beekeepers take care of the bees and harvest the honey.

Beekeepers wear protective clothing when they work around bees. Coveralls, veils and gloves protect them from bee stings.

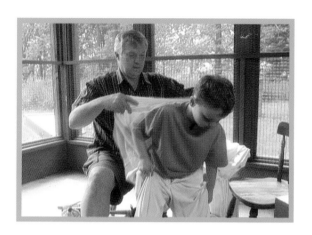

Bees can't see light colors or white very well, so beekeepers wear mostly white. If the bees get angry and look for something to sting, they won't land on Daniel!

Groups of bees are called colonies. Tens of thousands of bees make up a colony.

Whoa! That's a lot of bees!

Each colony has its own hive. In the wild, bees make their hives in hollowed-out trees or other out-of-the-way places.

On a bee farm, or apiary, bees live in man-made hives that look like stacked boxes.

In each hive you'll find wooden frames. The frames hold sheets of wax that the bees build honeycomb on. Honeycomb is made up of many tiny, six-sided rooms, or cells. Some cells hold bee eggs. Others hold honey or pollen. Allan opens a hive for Daniel to take a closer look.

First I puff some smoke on the hive with a smoker. Smoke calms the bees so they won't get angry!

Next Allan pulls
out a frame.
It's covered
in honeycomb
and bees.

Take a closer look
... fresh honey!

Colonies are made up of three kinds of honeybees: queens, drones and workers. There is only one queen in each colony, but there are hundreds of drones and thousands of workers. With so many bees in a hive, it can be hard to tell them apart. But look closely — you'll soon spot some differences.

This is Queen Maria. Beekeepers sometimes mark the queen with color so that she's easier to find.

The queen bee is the largest bee in the colony. Her body is long and slim.

Drones are the second-largest bees. They are males with very big eyes and thick bodies.

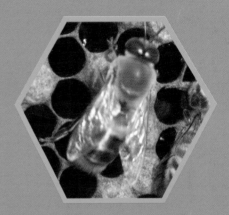

Workers are the smallest bees. Like the queen, they are slim females.

Each bee has a special job. The queen's job is to lay eggs. The drones' job is to mate with the queen.

Workers have many different jobs. Some workers stay in the hive. They take care of the baby bees and the queen, clean the hive and build cells, or guard the entrance. They are called house bees. Other workers go out to search for food. They are called foragers.

These are very
busy bees!

Foragers make many trips a day, visiting hundreds of flowers each time. Have you ever seen a bee climb into a flower? It gathers two kinds of food there: nectar and pollen. It sucks up the sweet nectar with its long tongue and stores it in a second stomach called a honey stomach.

I like to carry snacks in my pockets, too!

Pollen sticks to the bee's hairy body. The bee scrapes the pollen into baskets on its back legs and carries it back to the hive.

Back at the hive, the bees eat some of the nectar, but most of it is made into honey.

How do they do that?

First the house bees take the nectar from the foragers and swallow it. The nectar begins to change into honey in their honey stomachs. It's then put in an empty cell.

Once the cell is full and the nectar has completely transformed into honey, the house bees seal the cell with wax.

Pollen is also stored in cells. It's used to feed the baby bees.

Empty cells

Pollen-filled cells

Cells sealed with wax

Honey-filled cells! Yum!

Foragers also bring back information. They tell each other where to find flowers by doing dances over the honeycomb. A round dance means there are flowers nearby. A waggle dance means the flowers are far away. The waggle dance also shows which direction to follow and how far to fly.

Round Dance   Waggle Dance

Foragers work together because the more nectar they bring back, the more honey the bees will have for the winter.

Finally it's time to harvest the honey!

The beekeeper removes the frames from the hive and gently pushes the bees off with a bee brush. Then he cuts open the honeycomb with a thin knife and places the frames in a machine called an extractor.

The extractor spins the frames to shake the honey from the honeycomb.

Then the beekeeper pours the honey from this tap.

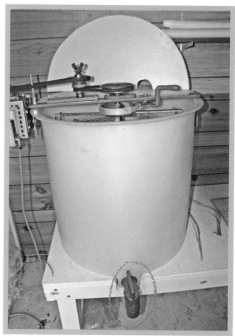

BEE-licious!

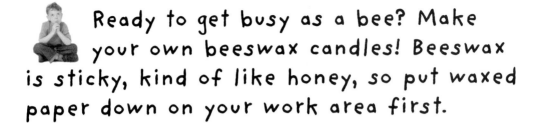
Ready to get busy as a bee? Make your own beeswax candles! Beeswax is sticky, kind of like honey, so put waxed paper down on your work area first.

You will need
- sheets of beeswax
- candlewick
- waxed paper
- scissors
- cookie cutters

1. With a grown-up's help, use a cookie cutter to cut 20 shapes from the beeswax.

2. One shape at a time, press 10 shapes together. Set aside. Repeat with the other 10 shapes.

3. Cut a piece of candlewick 2.5 cm (1 in.) longer than the height of your shape at its middle.

4. Lay the candlewick across the middle of one shape stack. The wick ends should hang off the stack's edges.

5. Lay the other shape stack on top of the candlewick and press the stacks together. Close-cut the wick at the bottom of your candle. Trim the wick at the top to 0.5 cm ($^1\!/_4$ in.).

Remember, always ask a grown-up to light a candle, and never leave a lit candle unattended.

Based on the TV series *This is Daniel Cook*. Concept created by J.J. Johnson and Blair Powers. Produced by marblemedia and Sinking Ship Productions Inc.

THIS IS DANIEL COOK, EPS #153 "Beekeeping" written by J.J. Johnson © 2004 Short Order Cook TV I Inc.

Kids Can Press acknowledges the financial support of the Government of Ontario, through the Ontario Media Development Corporation's Ontario Book Initiative; the Ontario Arts Council; the Canada Council for the Arts; and the Government of Canada, through the BPIDP, for our publishing activity.

The producers of *This is Daniel Cook* acknowledge the support of Treehouse TV, TVOntario, other broadcast and funding partners and the talented, hard-working crew that made *This is Daniel Cook* a reality. In addition, they acknowledge the support and efforts of Deb, Murray and the Cook family, as well as Karen Boersma, Sheila Barry and Valerie Hussey at Kids Can Press.

Published in Canada by
Kids Can Press Ltd.
29 Birch Avenue
Toronto, ON M4V 1E2

Published in the U.S. by
Kids Can Press Ltd.
2250 Military Road
Tonawanda, NY 14150

www.kidscanpress.com

Written by Yvette Ghione
Edited by Karen Li
Illustrations and design by Céleste Gagnon
With special thanks to Allan Foster and Peter Nixon
of the Kortright Centre for Conservation

Printed and bound in Singapore

The hardcover edition of this book is smyth sewn casebound.
The paperback edition of this book is limp sewn with a drawn-on cover.

Kids Can Press is a LORUS™ Entertainment company

CM 07 0 9 8 7 6 5 4 3 2 1
CM PA 07 0 9 8 7 6 5 4 3 2 1

Visit Daniel online at **www.thisisdanielcook.com**

Library and Archives Canada Cataloguing in Publication

Ghione, Yvette

This is Daniel Cook making honey / written by Yvette Ghione

ISBN-13: 978-1-55453-085-4 (bound)
ISBN-10: 1-55453-085-7 (bound)
ISBN-13: 978-1-55453-086-1 (pbk.)
ISBN-10: 1-55453-086-5 (pbk.)

1. Honey—Juvenile literature. 2. Bee culture—Juvenile literature.
I. Title.

SF523.5.G49 2007   j638'.16   C2006-902263-1

Photo Credits